Blast Zone

The Eruption
and Recovery of
Mount St. Helens

by David Stienecker

CELEBRATION PRESS
Pearson Learning Group

Contents

A Sleeping Giant

Mount St. Helens has stood for thousands of years in the southwestern part of Washington State. On May 18, 1980, an earthquake shook this majestic mountain and set off a terrible chain of events.

The eruption of Mount St. Helens sent huge clouds of ash and rock high into the sky.

An avalanche of rock and ice fell down the mountain's side, burying houses in its path. Hot gases that had been trapped inside the mountain exploded. The explosion sent a blast of hot rocks, steam, and gas sweeping over the forests below, leveling the trees. Ash, gases, and rock shot 12 miles (19 kilometers) into the sky. A heavy blanket of ash fell across the land and covered everything in sight. A sleeping giant had awakened.

Mount St. Helens had a record of volcanic activity that stretched far into its past. Native American people of the Northwest had long known of the mountain's fiery power.

The Klickitat people had called it Louwala-Clough. The name means "smoking mountain." In legends about Louwala-Clough, two brothers who were both in love with the same woman battled each other. They threw hot rocks at each other and caused earthquakes.

The mountain was named Mount St. Helens in 1792. A British sea captain was exploring the coast of the Pacific Northwest. When he saw the mountain from his ship, he decided to name it after the British ambassador to Spain, Baron St. Helens.

Around 1800, Native Americans saw a major eruption and reported it to settlers. Then, in the mid-1800s, the mountain began a series of explosions that continued on and off for years.

A witness, J. Parrish, wrote about an eruption in 1842. He said, "Vast columns of lurid smoke and fire . . . spread out in a line parallel to the . . . horizon, and presented the appearance of a vast table, supported by immense pillars of . . . flame and smoke." The last eruption came in 1857. Then the mountain quieted. It remained **dormant**, or inactive, until 1980.

Major volcanoes of the Cascade Range, which was formed by volcanic activity millions of years ago

Mount St. Helens is part of the Cascade Range. This chain of mountains is about 700 miles (1,125 kilometers) long. It goes from northern California through the states of Oregon and Washington and into southern British Columbia in Canada.

Many of the highest peaks in the Cascade Range are volcanoes. Some are **extinct**, but others are thought of as active because there are records of their eruptions. One volcano in the Cascades, Lassen Peak, had a huge eruption in 1915. Lassen is in California.

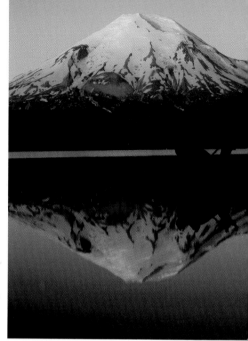

Mount St. Helens was considered one of the most beautiful mountains in the Cascades.

Before 1980, Mount St. Helens had been a beautiful, snow-capped mountain, rich with forests and wildlife. In the spring, wildflowers covered the mountain's slopes. Deer, elk, and bear roamed its forests. Songbirds added their music to the landscape.

At the base of the mountain lay Spirit Lake. The cold, clear waters of the lake were home to numerous fish. The water reflected the peak's near-perfect cone shape. The peak was sometimes compared to Mt. Fuji in Japan, one of the world's most beautiful mountains.

Many people thought Mount St. Helens and the area around it was the ideal spot for hiking and camping. Few thought that the mountain would ever erupt.

Warning Signals

A volcano is an opening in the earth's crust. The cone shape that we think of when we picture a volcano has built up from material that poured out from this opening. Through it, melted red-hot rock, gases, or ash can erupt, often violently.

Eruptions occur when **molten** rock, which has formed within the earth's crust, begins to rise. The melted rock moves up toward the surface. Solid rock that lies in the path of the rising molten rock can crack, causing earthquakes.

On March 20, 1980, an earthquake struck Mount St. Helens. It was the first signal that there was a problem on the mountain. There were more and more earthquakes in the next few days. In one two-day period, hundreds of quakes were recorded. People who lived near the volcano could feel some of these.

Scientists who were trying to measure these shocks could hardly keep track of them. One group of scientists said the mountain was "shaking like a mound of jelly." Then, on the afternoon of March 27, the mountain erupted.

A cloud of ash and steam blasted out of the top of Mount St. Helens. A crater formed that was about 250 feet across and 150 feet deep (76 by 46 meters). The earthquakes and eruptions went on. Then, a second crater formed. Finally, the two joined and formed a single, huge crater.

By early April, a new series of quakes were being recorded. Their steady movements told scientists that melted rock called **magma** was moving under the earth's surface. They were afraid the magma would erupt at any moment.

The governor of Washington at the time, Dixy Lee Ray, called a state of emergency. The roads leading to the mountain were closed. Some people didn't believe there was any danger. They complained that they couldn't get close enough to see what was going on.

The next few weeks were fairly calm. There were small eruptions from time to time. There was one very troubling sign, though. A bulge was forming on the mountain's north side. It grew at the rate of about 5 feet (1.5 meters) a day, until it stuck out more than 450 feet (137 meters).

The danger zone around the volcano was called the red zone. Because the volcano might erupt at any minute, people were being **evacuated** from the red zone.

Pressure from the magma inside Mount St. Helens caused a bulge to form on the north side of the mountain.

Harry Truman was an 83-year-old man who ran a lodge on Spirit Lake. He shared the same name as a U.S. president. This Harry had once met the more famous Truman. That had happened back when the famous Truman was the vice president under President Franklin D. Roosevelt. Harry said he had lived at the foot of Mount St. Helens for more than 50 years. He wasn't about to leave now. He told reporters, "I'm going to stay right here. . . . I'm part of that mountain."

By the middle of May, about 10,000 earthquakes had been recorded. Scientists knew the quakes were concentrated below the bulge on the mountain's north side.

On May 12, a large earthquake shook part of an ice field loose above Spirit Lake. It set off an avalanche 800 feet (244 meters) wide. Rock tumbled down the mountain and stopped just short of the lake.

A geologist named David Johnston worked at an observation station called Coldwater II on the north side. Johnston had a doctorate in geology, and he was an expert on the subject of Mount St. Helens. He knew the volcano was going to erupt. Knowing the danger, Johnston had still volunteered to collect samples from the crater.

On Saturday, May 17, Johnston said, "It could be in hours or even days or even a couple of months. But right now there's a very great hazard [on] the north side. . . . This is not a good spot to be standing in."

The mountain seemed to quiet down that day. The limits around the red zone were lifted for a few hours. That gave people who lived inside the zone a chance to collect their property. Some people felt they needed more time. The sheriff said they could come back the next morning at 10:00. Harry Truman still refused to leave.

At his post, David Johnston continued to observe the mountain. The next day, May 18, at 8:32 A.M., Johnston shouted into his two-way radio, "Vancouver! Vancouver! This is it!" Those were his last words.

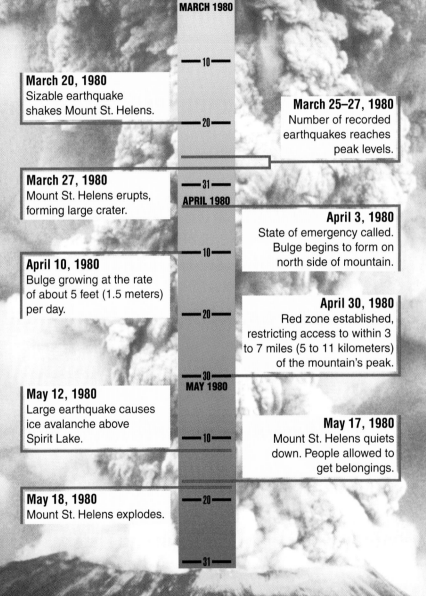

MARCH 1980

— 10 —

March 20, 1980
Sizable earthquake
shakes Mount St. Helens.

March 25–27, 1980
Number of recorded
earthquakes reaches
peak levels.

— 20 —

March 27, 1980
Mount St. Helens erupts,
forming large crater.

— 31 —
APRIL 1980

April 3, 1980
State of emergency called.
Bulge begins to form on
north side of mountain.

— 10 —

April 10, 1980
Bulge growing at the rate
of about 5 feet (1.5 meters)
per day.

— 20 —

April 30, 1980
Red zone established,
restricting access to within 3
to 7 miles (5 to 11 kilometers)
of the mountain's peak.

— 30 —
MAY 1980

May 12, 1980
Large earthquake causes
ice avalanche above
Spirit Lake.

May 17, 1980
Mount St. Helens quiets
down. People allowed to
get belongings.

— 10 —

May 18, 1980
Mount St. Helens explodes.

— 20 —

— 31 —

11

The Mountain Explodes

On the morning of May 18, two geologists, Keith and Dorothy Stoffel, were flying over Mount St. Helens. They wanted to check the crater to see how active it was. They arrived over the restricted area at 7:50 A.M. and flew over the crater twice. At first, it didn't look like an active volcano at all. Then Keith Stoffel noticed some **debris** moving down the mountainside. Suddenly, the whole north side of the mountain began sliding away.

An earthquake with a magnitude of 5.1 on the **Richter scale** had broken loose the bulge on the side of the mountain. The resulting **avalanche**, or landslide, was the largest one in recorded history. It suddenly reduced the pressure on the rock that had been covering the magma inside the mountain.

It was like opening a pressure valve. Super-hot water and gases were instantly released in a tremendous explosion that ripped through the north face of the mountain. A huge blast of black smoke and ash shot out sideways. As the blast surged from the volcano, it carried with it the rock it had shattered.

The landslide set off a huge sideways blast of gas, steam, ash, and rock.

The force of the sideways explosion formed a column inside the mountain. This caused a second explosion that went straight up from the mountain's peak. It threw hot ash, rocks, smoke, and gas 12 miles (19 kilometers) into the sky.

With massive force, the first blast sent a huge, rolling cloud of gas, steam, and rock down the slopes of the mountain. Moving even faster than the avalanche, the deadly cloud swept over the land at speeds of nearly 700 miles per hour (mph), or about 1,129 kilometers per hour (kph). Heat in the cloud rose to nearly 600° Fahrenheit (300° Celsius). Large stands of trees that lay in the cloud's path—the "blast zone"—were knocked over like matchsticks.

People at the base of the mountain began to feel the falling ash and rock. One of the people caught in the ashfall was a TV news photographer, David Crockett. He had been taking pictures on a logging road when the mountain erupted.

Choking as he talked into a tape recorder, Crockett said how hard it was to breathe through the blizzard of ash. He thought he was going to die, but amazingly, he made it out. His film of the disaster was shown widely on television.

Meanwhile, the avalanche continued to thunder down the mountain's side. Heading north, the landslide hit the valley of the North Fork Toutle River. Then it split into three sections.

Forests surrounding the volcano were covered in ash.

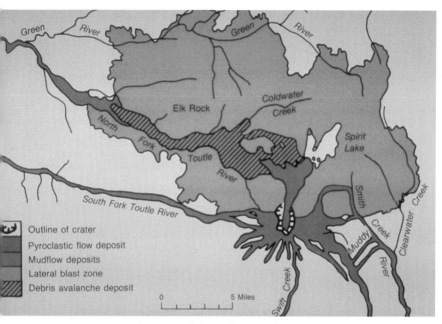

The path of the volcano's damage

Key:
- Outline of crater
- Pyroclastic flow deposit
- Mudflow deposits
- Lateral blast zone
- Debris avalanche deposit

0   5 Miles

The largest part slid down the river for nearly 14 miles (22 kilometers). A second part plunged into Spirit Lake, causing monster waves and filling the lake with floating trees and rock debris. The last part of the avalanche traveled over a ridge and flowed into South Coldwater Creek.

As the hot material mixed with water, it formed **mudflows** that choked the local rivers. At one point, the Toutle River rose about 21 feet (7 meters) above its normal level. The material was around 90° Fahrenheit (32° Celsius). That was hot enough to kill all the fish in the Toutle River.

Mike and Lu Moore and their two children were camped on the north face of the volcano. Suddenly, they heard a low rumble. A dark cloud loomed overhead. Mike and Lu quickly carried their children to a nearby hunter's shack.

The Moores wet socks for themselves and their children to breathe through. They waited as ash and rock pounded the shack. When the ash storm ended, the Moores went outside to find an ash-filled land where the forest had once stood. Forced to camp overnight, they were rescued by a helicopter the next day.

There was more destruction to come. Around noon, people could see that the volcano was erupting with a super-hot mix of rock, ash, and gas.

This **pyroclastic flow** rushed down the sides of the mountain. It reached temperatures of nearly 800° Fahrenheit (427° Celsius) and moved so rapidly that its force threw trucks into the air.

At the end of the day, what had once been a hikers' dream place had been reduced to a wasteland. Forest and wildlife had been damaged in an area of over 200 square miles (518 square kilometers).

Tragically, 57 people had lost their lives. Some had suffocated or died of burns. Others were buried in the mud and ash.

Search and Rescue

Almost immediately after Mount St. Helens erupted, the Air Force, U.S. Forest Service, and National Guard began search and rescue efforts. Ash and debris from the avalanche had blocked many roads, so much of the search was conducted by helicopter.

Helicopters flew low over the blast zone, looking for people to rescue. Some had been stranded after mudflows or logjams wiped out roads and bridges. Others had been caught in rising floods. Some had been walking for hours through the mounds of ash. Many were worn out from breathing in the ash. Campers, hikers, and other survivors waved desperately to the helicopters flying over them.

Helicopters were used to search for survivors after the Mount St. Helens eruption.

Sadly, one person who would never be rescued was David Johnston, the young geologist who sounded the alarm when Mount St. Helens began erupting.

The eruption's blast had made a direct hit on Johnston's observation station at Coldwater II. When rescue helicopters flew over his campsite, there was nothing left to be seen. The entire area was covered in hot ash. Rescuers searched for Johnston's body, but never found it.

Harry Truman also died on his beloved mountain. His lodge on Spirit Lake had been directly in the path of the avalanche. When rescuers flew over his home, they saw that it had been buried beneath hundreds of feet of ash and debris. Harry Truman had died almost instantly.

While the survivors mourned those who had died, they knew that the loss of lives could have been much worse. A day before, loggers had been at work in the blast zone. Later in the day, more property owners would have been at Spirit Lake, getting their belongings. The roadblocks had kept many people from entering the blast zone. Considering the difficulties they faced, the pilots had also done a remarkable job of saving people. Their maps didn't help them much because of the drastic changes in the landscape. They didn't even know whom they were searching for.

Wildlife was devastated by the blast.

Wildlife in the area was devastated by the blast. Ash smothered the animals and plants on the ground. Many birds and insects burned in the air as they tried to fly to safety. The Washington State Department of Game put the number of large mammals killed at about 7,000. That included deer, bear, and elk.

In all, scientists thought that millions of birds and mammals died. They included elk, deer, bear, mountain lions, rabbits, pheasants, ducks, geese, bobcats, and raccoons. Millions more fish were killed.

The Aftermath

What did the area around Mount St. Helens look like after the blast? First, there were the changes to the majestic mountain itself.

Before it erupted, Mount St. Helens had risen 9,677 feet (2,950 meters) above sea level. About thirteen hundred feet (400 meters) of mountain had been removed by the eruption. Mount St. Helens now stood at 8,365 feet (2,550 meters). So much earth had exploded, there was now a horseshoe-shaped crater about 1 mile (1.6 kilometers) wide.

As mudflows had surged down the Toutle River, they pushed walls of water ahead of them. The river flooded. The water destroyed bridges, swept away homes, and killed thousands of animals. As the mudflows continued down the river, cut timber and fallen trees piled up. The logs became so tightly packed that people used them to walk across the river.

The upper half of Spirit Lake also filled up with mud and trees. Thousands of floating trees covered the lake's surface. Debris raised the lakebed by nearly 300 feet (91 meters). In the Columbia River, the bed was raised so high that many ships were stranded in their ports.

The force of the volcanic blast snapped off trees as if they were matchsticks.

Hundreds of miles of highways and roads had been destroyed. So were 27 bridges and nearly 200 houses and cabins. Many more homes were damaged by the avalanche, mudflows, and flooding. People who had been lucky to escape death were left homeless.

Millions of grown trees had been snapped off or uprooted. Almost all of the fallen trees pointed in the same direction—away from the blast.

President Jimmy Carter flew over the area. "I've never seen anything like it," he said. "The Moon looks like a golf course compared to what's up there."

Tons of ash fell on the city of Yakima.

In the towns around the immediate area of the blast, day turned to night as ash began to fall. The ash plume that had risen miles into the air was coming down.

Yakima, Washington, lies 85 miles (137 kilometers) away from Mount St. Helens. At 9:30 on the morning of Sunday, May 18, a cloud of darkness fell over Yakima. Soft, gray ash began to descend.

Ash filled the streets and crept inside people's houses. The town's water treatment plant became clogged. Fields of hay and alfalfa were flattened by the ash. Cars stalled.

Alarmed at the possible damage to their health, the people of Yakima put on face masks. They were told to stay indoors so they wouldn't breathe the ash. Schools and businesses closed. So did many highways and roads. Drivers couldn't see through the falling ash.

Cleaning up the tons of ash that covered the city of Yakima was a long, dirty job. In all, about 600,000 tons of ash were hauled away.

Winds carried the ash to the north and east. An estimated 540 million tons of ash fell on more than 22,000 square miles (57,000 square kilometers) of Earth. Over the days and weeks that followed the eruption, the ash spread beyond Washington State to parts of Idaho, Montana, Canada, New Mexico, and Wyoming. It fell across midwestern states, too. Ash was even recorded in New York, Pennsylvania, and South Carolina.

Lighter amounts of ash rose high into the atmosphere and drifted across the Atlantic Ocean, Europe, and Asia. Scientists thought bits of ash might stay in the atmosphere for two or more years. However, the ash was not as destructive as scientists had feared. Most of it dropped back to Earth quickly, and it didn't affect the weather. It even had some good effects. The ash helped to keep moisture in the ground. This was good for the wheat crop on farms that had a heavy ashfall, since wheat plants need moisture.

VOLCANIC EXPLOSIVITY INDEX (VEI)

VEI	Description	Volume of Ejected Material (km³= cubic kilometers)	Height of Plume	Duration	Example (date of eruption)
0	Non-Explosive	varies	less than 100 m	varies	Mt. Kilauea (currently active)
1	Small	less than .001 km³	100–1,000 m	less than 1 hour	Nyiragongo (1982)
2	Moderate	.001–.01 km³	1–5 km	1–6 hours	Galeras (1992)
3	Moderate/ Large	.01–.1 km³	3–15 km	1–12 hours	Ruiz (1985)
4	Large	.1–1 km³	10–25 km	1–12 hours	Kelut, Indonesia (1990)
5	Very Large	1–10 km³	more than 25 km	6–12 hours	Mount St. Helens (1982) and Vesuvius (A.D. 79)
6	Very Large	10–100 km³	more than 25 km	more than 12 hours	Krakatau (1883)
7	Very Large	100–1,000 km³	more than 25 km	more than 12 hours	Tambora (1815)
8	Very Large	more than 1,000 km³	more than 25 km	more than 12 hours	Yellowstone Caldera (2 million years ago)

How does the eruption of Mount St. Helens compare to other volcanic eruptions? To help answer that question, scientists propose using a scale called the Volcanic Explosivity Index (VEI). It looks at the things that can be observed about an eruption. These include how long the eruption lasts and how much material is thrown out. By these measures, Mount St. Helens was a very large eruption. It had a VEI of 5.

The eruption of Mount Vesuvius in A.D. 79 buried the city of Pompeii for over a thousand years.

To compare eruptions, however, scientists must also look at how much damage they cause. By this measure, Mount St. Helens was a modest eruption. The number of lives lost in the disaster—57 people—could have been much worse. Some historic eruptions have buried entire cities. This happened when Mount Vesuvius erupted in A.D. 79 and buried the city of Pompeii in ash.

Other eruptions have caused deadly tidal waves. Such an eruption occurred in Krakatau, Indonesia, in 1883. The explosions could be heard 2,000 miles (3,226 kilometers) away. They set off tidal waves that killed 36,000 people.

Mount St. Helens may have been a small eruption compared to others, yet it caused terrible damage to plants and animals. Could the area ever recover?

Recovery Begins

It's hard to believe that anything could have survived the intense temperatures and forces inside the blast zone on May 18, 1980. The first scientists to enter the blast zone saw a brown and gray, ash-covered land. Surprisingly, however, many living things did survive. Over time, new plants and animals joined them.

Large mammals did not survive in the blast zone, but some small ones, like the northern pocket gopher, lived. The survivors had been sheltered under snow or below ground. In all, 14 species of small mammals are known to have survived. These

The northern pocket gopher was one of the animals that survived underground.

26

included chipmunks and white-footed deer mice.

Many insects died when tiny pieces of ash became trapped in their body hair. The sharp pieces of ash cut away at the insects' hard covering. They lost moisture and died.

Ash killed countless bees and ladybugs. However, ants underground had survived. Eggs that other insects had laid underground survived, too. Tiny insects such as mites that were hidden deep inside rotting logs also lived.

After the eruption, these animals went on with their lives. Pocket gophers started burrowing, pushing up soil from beneath the ash layer. This rich soil was needed for seeds to grow. Ants came out of their underground colonies and began scurrying around looking for food. Frogs that had gone into a sleeplike state during the eruption woke up and began to croak.

Then the colonizers arrived—animals that moved in from other areas. By the spring of 1981, birds began returning to the area. So did flying insects and spiders carried by the wind. Animals such as squirrels and mice that were not too picky about where they lived and what they ate came, too. Large mammals such as deer and elk were seen moving around blown-down trees just a few days after the disaster.

The fireweed plant sprouted through the ash.

Colonizers came because there was food for them to eat. Though layers of ash had killed or buried many plants, some types survived. Some seeds, roots, and bulbs were still alive after the eruption. Like the small animals, they had been buried deep underground. Dirt and snow had protected them.

Soon after the eruption, scientists found fireweed sprouts poking through cracks in the hardened ash. The fireweed spread, and animals moved in to eat it. The growing fireweed plants broke up the hardened ash crust. This made it easier for other plants to grow there.

Plants that had died helped make the ash a better place for new plants to grow. Seeds blew in and sprouted. One of the earliest plants to take hold in the blast zone was called lupine. Grasses, clover, and other plants began to grow, too. Elk and other animals that grazed on the plants came back to the blast zone.

Over 20 years have passed since the 1980 eruption. One of the biggest changes in the landscape has come from the new types of trees and shrubs that have moved into the area. Winds carried the seeds of these plant colonizers from forests miles away. Scientists guess that by the year 2100, scattered groups of trees will begin to merge. The land will look like a forest once again.

Roosevelt elk began returning to the blast zone as soon as there were plants to eat.

A Living Laboratory

In 1982, President Ronald Reagan signed a law creating the Mount St. Helens National Volcanic Monument. It opened to visitors in 1983. The monument covers 110,000 acres of land that was damaged or destroyed by the 1980 eruption.

Inside the monument, the land is recovering naturally from the disaster. It has become a living laboratory. Scientists and visitors alike can learn how nature recovers after a volcanic eruption.

Millions of people have visited the National Volcanic Monument. There are spectacular views where people can observe and learn how the landscape and the volcano are changing.

Scientists continue to keep a close watch on Mount St. Helens. It is still an active volcano—and

Views of the mountain in 1980 (left) and in 1984 (right).

possibly, a dangerous one. Since 1980, there have been dozens of small eruptions and many minor earthquakes. Scientists keep track of each event from a volcano observatory in Vancouver, Washington. The observatory is named for David Johnston. Its staff watches Mount St. Helens and the other volcanoes in the Cascade Range.

In 1998 and again in 2001, there were groups of earthquakes. In each event, hundreds of quakes were recorded. They did not result in an eruption, however. The mountain seems to have settled down.

Since the 1980 eruption, a new lava dome has grown in the center of the volcano's crater. Each new eruption pushes lava up from the bottom of the crater. It acts like a tube of toothpaste that keeps squeezing new material up and over old material. Today the lava dome is about 1,000 feet (305 meters) high and still slowly growing.

Mount St. Helens seems to be rebuilding itself from the inside. One day it may again be covered with forests and topped with a glistening white cap of snow.

Glossary

avalanche — a large mass of snow, ice, mud, or rocks sliding down the side of a mountain

colonizers — plants and animals that move into one area from another area

debris — a buildup of rock fragments and other materials

dormant — in a state of inactivity

evacuated — to be removed from an area

extinct — no longer existing

magma — the very hot, melted rock beneath the earth's crust

molten — made liquid by heat

mudflows — mixtures of volcanic material, earth, and water

pyroclastic flow — avalanche of hot ash, pumice, rock fragments, and volcanic gases

Richter scale — scale used for measuring the force of an earthquake in terms of energy

volcano — an opening in the earth's crust through which melted rock, gases, or ash is expelled, often violently